HULL CORPORATION BUSES

Malcolm Wells and Paul Morfitt

AMBERLEY

First published 2017

Amberley Publishing
The Hill, Stroud
Gloucestershire, GL5 4EP

www.amberley-books.com

Copyright © Malcolm Wells and Paul Morfitt,
2017

The right of Malcolm Wells and Paul Morfitt
to be identified as the Authors of this work has
been asserted in accordance with the Copyrights,
Designs and Patents Act 1988.

ISBN 978 1 4456 6754 6 (print)
ISBN 978 1 4456 6755 3 (ebook)

British Library Cataloguing in Publication Data.
A catalogue record for this book is available from
the British Library.

Origination by Amberley Publishing.
Printed in the UK.

Foreword

Kingston upon Hull's municipal buses served the city (mostly) with distinction from 1909 until 1994. In that time over 900 buses and coaches were owned, so attempting to provide an appropriate selection of photographs that conveys the essentials of Hull's operations has proved difficult; even more so given that the authors had over 2,000 views from which to choose.

We have tried to show the buses in their natural habitats all around the city, from initial routes within the inner city to the far-flung estate routes of later years – not to mention post-deregulation suburban and rural excursions. In addition we have tried to cover as many classes of vehicles as possible and we have attempted to avoid (mostly) photographs that have been published elsewhere and official views.

From 1960 onwards the selection leans heavily on Malcolm's own photographs but we have also used some photographs that have been acquired. Wherever possible we have acknowledged or attempted to trace the photographer but many views do not carry any indication of their origin and we apologise if anyone sees one of their own without due acknowledgement.

There is a caveat about delivery and withdrawal dates, especially pre-Second World War dates since the destruction of the head office and its replacement in 1941 destroyed many records, which even extensive research has not been able to replace. Some sources contain errors, which mainly arise from this problem

We would like to thank Mick Nicholson and Paul Gibson for contributing pre-war views from their collections, as well as the late Les Storry and Geoff O'Connell for photographs.

Introduction

In 1909 Hull's tramway system comprised 116 trams running on seven routes. Powers existed for a tramway along Cleveland Street to Stoneferry Green. The Council was reluctant to build this since most of the route would serve industrial works and decided to use motorbuses even though it would lose money. Six buses, which were purchased from the Mersey Railway Company, opened the route on 29 July 1909 from North Bridge. The losses mounted so it ceased on 5 April 1913.

Not until October 1921 did motorbus operation re-start, running via densely populated areas around Charles Street and Barmston Street to Stoneferry Green.

The next route (March 1923) served the Garden Village area (built by James Reckitt for his workers). In October a route opened from the city centre to the Fish Dock, which continued via St George's Road, Albert Avenue and Sculcoates Lane to Stoneferry. This was soon divided into the City – Fish Dock and Fish Dock – Stoneferry sections, the latter immortalised with the 'Fish Dock Bus' title. It enabled workers and school children to avoid the city centre and two journeys. October also saw a route to Preston Road via Newbridge Road. The late twenties routes to Boothferry Road and Stoneferry via Cleveland Street were started.

By 1930 the bus fleet numbered fifty compared with the trams' 179. Proposals to introduce trolleybuses were rejected by voters in 1929 and 1930, with an order for twelve Guy trolleybuses being replaced with one for motorbuses.

In 1931 a motorbus-minded Duncan P. Morrison came from Dundee. He condemned the tramway system and introduced a blue and white livery based on Dundee colours. The remaining open top and outside staircase buses were replaced with a mixture of hired and purchased buses, mainly from Daimler and Leyland.

More routes beyond the tramway termini were opened in May 1930 (Sutton via two routes), along with Willerby Road (June) and Hall Road (July), followed by Greenwood Avenue in 1933. The Pier tram route was replaced in September 1931 followed by the Holderness Road tram 'TH' in June 1932.

From 27 February 1933 all Sunday morning and late night tram services were replaced with several bus routes that operated across the city centre, with cross-city workings being confined solely to these journeys.

In July 1934 a coordination agreement with East Yorkshire Motor Services was introduced. Hull and the surrounding area was divided into an inner area (designated 'A'), in which the Corporation received all fares income, a 'B' area comprising mainly the rest of the city where mileage and fares were equally shared and a 'C' area, the preserve of EYMS.

The outer sections of some tram routes were replaced by seven new bus routes – Pickering Road, Anlaby Common, Greenwood Avenue via Bricknell Avenue, Hall Road via Cottingham Road and two routes to Sutton Annexe and Ings Road via Garden Village. Ten Leyland and twenty Daimler buses entered service after several months' storage.

All the radial routes started from streets within the city centre. To relieve congestion some were transferred in 1933 to an area alongside the Electricity Department's head offices in Ferensway. A new bus station adjoining Paragon Railway Station designated the 'Coach Station' opened on 22 September 1935 together with a new central bus garage and parking area. Buses continued to run via Paragon Street and Jameson Street.

In 1935 Duncan Morrison was succeeded by his assistant Jack Lawson. He started to replace the remaining trams with trolleybuses (Hedon Road excepted) and introduced the streamlined azure and white livery that was to last for another thirty years.

Thirty-five Daimler and twenty AEC chassis arrived in 1938/9. Plans for twenty buses annually for the next three years were thwarted by the outbreak of war, as was the plan to convert two motorbus routes to trolleybus operation.

Meanwhile, new services to Hedon and Paull outside the city boundary following the joint purchase of Sharpe's Motors were started. A works service between Queens Hotel (on Princes Avenue) and Chapman Street commenced on 2 December 1937. Routes to new housing areas at Setting Dyke (March 1937), Wold Road and Bilton Grange followed in 1937/38.

An immediate result of the outbreak of war was the withdrawal of night services and the Witty Street route. Mr Lawson suffered a fatal heart attack in November 1939. The Electricity Department Manager, Mr Bellamy, was placed temporarily in charge and not until March 1941 did G. H. Pulfrey from St Helens commence work.

The department had surplus buses since government policy forbade disposal of vehicles without permission, so it was able to lend buses to London Passenger Transport Board, Coventry and Sheffield in 1940/1.

To reduce mileage, two transfer schemes were introduced in 1940. Service 48 ran between Bilton Grange and trolleybus service 64 at Portobello Street (May). The second (in July) saw service 15 running between Greenwood Avenue and trolleybus services 61/61A at the Chanterlands Avenue/Bricknell Avenue junction, with the third (in July) service 16 from Greenwood Avenue and trolleybus service 63 terminus at Endike Lane. This arrangement, which operated between 9 a.m. and noon on weekdays, was abandoned later in the year.

On the night of 7/8 May 1941 the central bus garage was destroyed along with forty-four motorbuses, while twenty-one buses were damaged. Even buses (eighteen over two years) parked at various dispersal points were damaged at various times. Regent No. 144, which was slightly damaged at Central Garage on 31 March 1941 and at Pickering Park on 29 April, was totally destroyed on 7/8 May. Buses were borrowed from several Yorkshire operators. Seven Daimler CP6 buses were purchased from Wallasey Corporation, their dual entrance/exit bodies being converted to rear entrance by Halifax Corporation.

Hull was allocated ten AEC Regents – nine with austerity bodywork, the other (No. 196) having a Brush body intended for Coventry – and four Leyland TD7s to replace lost buses.

To deter short distance passengers from long distance buses, a limited stop system was implemented in 1941. The first setting down point was two stops beyond trolleybus or tram termini.

In May 1941 the white areas of the livery were painted over with blue to eliminate, it was claimed, the possibility of the white being seen from enemy aircraft. Concurrently it would appear that rear destination boxes were painted over.

1943 saw the introduction of ten buses using gas-producer trailers on services 21 and 22 to Cottingham Grove estate. They were disliked by passengers who found them to be very slow.

More wartime deliveries comprised thirty-six Guy Arabs carrying Massey, Duple or Park Royal bodies between 1946 and 1950 ninety-five AEC Regent IIs and IIIs together with six AEC Regals arrived. All pre-war vehicles were withdrawn giving a fleet of 146 double deckers and six single deckers. Twenty-four Massey and Weymann bodies were transferred to wartime chassis while others were refurbished.

Several received the new standard destination layout of two numbers above an aperture used to describe the main road along which the service ran. Others retained pre-war blinds, some with the Kelbus flap.

Six more Regents with concealed radiators arrived in 1953. The Department wanted twenty but was only given loan sanction for the six.

Post-war extensions to corporation housing estates included Sutton Road, Bricknell Avenue, Bilton Grange, Longhill and Greatfield.

The Regals were converted to one-man operation for two works services in east Hull. Ten AEC Reliances arrived in 1957/8 to permit one-man operation of routes 14/19. The first of an extensive network of school services (between Greatfield and Bricknell Avenue) started in May 1959.

Proposals to abandon the trolleybus system were confirmed in 1960. The first five of 247 Atlanteans arrived in May 1960 along with five more Reliances for OMO operations on services 26, 32 and 34.

During the 1960s new estates were opened at Orchard Park in the north, Boothferry in the west, Greatfield and Ings Road in the east and the first parts of the huge Bransholme estate in the north-east. In 1967 more inter-estate school and works services were introduced. In addition to annual deliveries of Atlanteans, second-hand buses came from Newcastle, St Helens, Leicester and Nottingham to replace wartime buses and to cover for extensive body repairs to the Regent III fleet. Twelve Leyland Panthers were received (an order for five more cancelled) as OMO was extended including the circular route.

In September 1969, double deck one-man operation started on the 20 group of routes. This was quickly expanded so that from November 1972 the entire network had been converted.

Throughout the seventies the Bransholme estate was greatly extended the longest route being eight miles with a journey time of 45 minutes. New vehicles appeared in the shape of Metropolitans and Metrobuses before a reversion to Atlanteans, after which Dennis and Scania supplied buses.

In 1982 a coaching arm was launched using three Plaxton-bodied Leylands in a white livery with blue and white strips as called 'KINGSTONIAN'.

The Corporation formed a limited company before deregulation in July 1986. This replaced all existing routes and reduced the fleet size from 230 to 140. Cottingham Road and Holderness Road garages (both full of withdrawn buses) were closed. In September the company won forty-seven school contracts but incredibly was short of serviceable buses and so borrowed buses from Grimsby-Cleethorpes and Nottingham and purchased seven Atlanteans from WYPTE. Fifteen minibuses in a tramway-inspired livery introduced three new services in 1987.

In response to competition from various independents, a low cost Citilink company was formed with buses in a two-tone green livery. Later buses transferred received an all-white livery.

Other moves included the purchase of York Pullman and two continental coach operators while the coaching side became a separate company in 1990.

In 1992 EYMS started some new local routes in competition, which brought retaliation with KHCT Ltd's new routes to Hessle, Willerby, Anlaby, Cottingham, Longhill and Withernsea.

It all came at a cost as financial pressures mounted. A new management team was brought in to concentrate on the local network and sell the acquired companies. Passenger numbers had fallen and it was no surprise when the 52 per cent of KHCT's holding was sold to Cleveland Transit in December 1993. This was followed by the sale to Stagecoach in 1994 and all trace of the once respected Corporation Transport began to disappear.

An admiring crowd views one of the six Saurers bought from the Mersey Railway Company for the Stoneferry route in 1909. All were withdrawn in March 1912. (Paul Gibson)

AEC '802' No. 3 with Fry O48RO bodywork was bought in 1921 for a revised route to Stoneferry. It served until 1931, having been renumbered 17. (Authors' collection)

No. 1 was an AEC 'K' used as a committee coach from 1921 and lasted in service until 1932. Its bodywork (B33R) builder is unknown. (G. M. O'Connell)

This view shows a Bristol (possibly No. 5) with EEC O54RO bodywork on the Preston Road service in Queen Victoria Square. Its career ran from February 1923 to December 1930. (Authors' collection)

In 1923, several Bristols with EEC bodies were placed in service, one of which is seen in Jameson Street outside Hammond's store. (Authors' collection)

A side view in Jameson Street outside Hammond's store of one of the Roe-bodied Bristol 'A's, believed to be No. 41. (Authors' collection)

No. 22 was a Commer with Barnaby B26D bodywork to a rather neat design. It was acquired from the 'Blue Bus Company' in October 1923. Some sources say it was re-bodied to B26F but no firm evidence has yet come to light. (Paul Gibson)

A deserted Newbridge Road is traversed by a Bristol shortly after the opening of the new route. (Authors' collection)

Believed to be No. 14 (later No. 24), this vehicle has a Guy chassis type BA or B with Guy B26 F body. It ran from December 1923 to December 1929 and was probably the first bus with pneumatic tyres. (Authors' collection)

Bristol 'A' No. 16 with Short H48RO body of 1927, seen with crew and other officials. Having a short life, it saw withdrawal in 1934. (Authors' collection)

A well-patronised outing sees five double deckers led by No. 42, a Bristol 'A' with Roe H50R bodywork of 1928. In 1935 its top deck was removed for conversion to a breakdown vehicle. (Paul Gibson)

No. 73, an AEC Regent with Brush H50R body, passes an unidentified bus in Jameson Street. Its career spanned 1932 to 1947. (Authors' collection)

Another view of AEC No. 73, this time in Paragon Street. Until route numbers were officially introduced this shows how the number blind was set. (East Pennine Transport Group)

One of the Brush-bodied FCXs seen in pouring rain in Paragon Street. Note the different application of the livery and position of the destination indicator. (HDM)

Five of the 1932 AEC Regals were bodied by Brush (B28D to a similar specification by English Electric). Here is No. 5. (Authors' collection)

Crew and Guy FCX No. 52 pose for the camera near the Preston Road terminus. Note the full window openings. It had a short life from February 1929 to December 1936. (Authors' collection)

Dennis HV No. 69 was delivered in May 1931 with Ransomes, Sims & Jeffries H51R bodywork. Alternative tenders for bodywork included provision for a door immediately behind the front axle but this was not adopted. After a short working life of just seven years No. 69 was converted to a mobile mortuary. (Authors' collection)

A pleasant scene at Sutton Church in the early thirties when Sutton was a small village surrounded by countryside. (Authors' collection)

All Leyland TD2 was originally on loan from Leyland Motors in 1932 and numbered 104. When purchased in 1943 it was renumbered 116. This bodywork featured a route number box and destination indicator at the front and a two-piece indicator over the platform. It was not withdrawn until late 1949. (East Pennine Transport Group)

An official view of AEC Regent No. 83 with English Electric H47R bodywork of 1932. This went to London and Sheffield in 1940/41 and was withdrawn in December 1948. (D. Bielby collection)

A rear view of the English Electric body on a Daimler CP6 chassis of 1934. This example was destroyed by bombing on 7/8 May 1941. (D. Bielby collection)

Leyland Titan No. 93 was on loan in 1931 and carried a crimson and cream livery on its Leyland lowbridge body. (Authors' collection)

Leyland Titan No. 115 with Leyland H51R bodywork dated from 1934. (East Pennine Transport Group)

Driver Alf Roberts and conductor Harry Taylor pose proudly at Pickering Road in front of what is probably Daimler CP6 No. 144 with Weymann H53R bodywork. No. 144 was damaged by bombing in March and again in April 1941 before being destroyed in the central garage on the night of 7/8 May 1941. (Authors' collection)

Leyland No. 107 was another loanee until purchased and renumbered 121. It is passing through Queen Victoria Square en route to Garden Village. (Authors' collection)

An official view of AEC 'Q' No. 127 with its MCCW H58F bodywork. It dates from 1933 and was sold in 1943. It was exhibited at the 1933 Commercial Motor Show and was on loan to London Transport from October 1940 to May 1941. A second 'Q', numbered 148 with Park Royal bodywork, was on loan from AEC in blue and white during 1934. (G. M. O'Connell)

Guy No. 48 is seen in Alfred Gelder Street returning from Suttoway. Note the 'A' just under the canopy, for which no explanation has been discovered. The rear of later FCX No. 58 can be seen with a board showing its destination under the rear lower deck window. (HDM)

This is the interior of the Central Bus Garage not long after opening in October 1935. (Kingston upon Hull History Centre)

Daimler CO5G No. 153 is in the Coach Station. This photograph shows the layout of the barriers. Nos 150-169 were the first buses in Jack Lawson's new streamline livery. No. 153 survived until December 1948 and later had a removable hatch in the cab for tuition purposes. (Authors' collection)

One of the 1932 AEC single deckers crosses Walton Street, crossing possibly on the Fish Dock Bus route. (M. Nicholson)

The rear of an unidentified bus with unusual black on white route number and destination blind. The location
is the Waterworks crossing on Spring Bank West. (M. Nicholson)

This and the next four
photographs were taken for the
Hull Daily Mail in 1936 to show
the congestion in Paragon Street,
which at that time still possessed
EYMS terminal points as well as
numerous KHCT stopping places.
They also convey the variations
in the livery and destination
indicators on different buses. Not
until 1941 were buses diverted
along Ferensway to save petrol and
tyre wear. (HDM)

Another view, this time taken from an upper floor of a building. (HDM)

The nearside bus is bound for Anlaby Common but shows Anlaby Park. (HDM)

A quieter view. (HDM)

A rare view of the AEC 'Q' in service, bound for Gipsyville Estate on service 7. (HDM)

Daimler CO5G No. 156 passes through Queen Victoria Square en route to Preston Road. No. 156 also survived the war. (Authors' collection)

One of the second batches of Daimlers that arrived in 1937 is posed in Queens Gardens. Note the revised destination indicator featuring a flap to show either the outward destination or the inward 'CITY'. (East Pennine Transport Group)

This shows part of the damage to the Central Bus Garage on the Short Street side. Massey-bodied AEC Regent No. 177 has the bottom part of the destination display flipped over to reveal the 'CITY' destination. (Authors' collection)

A wintry scene in 1943 with buses stabled where, until 7/8 May 1941, they would have been inside the Central Bus Garage. (P. Gibson)

AEC Regent No. 194 was one of ten received early in 1942 to replace vehicles lost on 7/8 May 1941. It carried a Utility Brush UH56R body in an all-blue livery with a full blind display at the front. No. 194 would receive the Massey body from AEC Regent No. 175 in 1949. (W. J. Haynes)

AEC Regent No. 196 was originally intended for Coventry Corporation but was diverted to Hull. It carried a Brush H60R body complete with standard Coventry destination layout. Note the unusual position of the 'CORPORATION TRANSPORT' rectangle. (W. J. Haynes)

In May 1941 the white areas of the livery on all buses and trolleybuses were over painted with blue to prevent their being seen from the air, as demonstrated on AEC Regent No. 78, which arrived in 1932. Brush H56R bodywork was carried. It was loaned to London Transport from October 1940 until May 1941. No. 78 lasted until 1947. (W. J. Haynes)

Clarence Street in July 1943 sees three buses, the one on the right being a Utility bus. The nearest is No. 126 (ex-No. 112), a Leyland TD2 with Leyland H48R bodywork. This and the one in front (a 1939 Massey-bodied Regent) have had the white painted over and rear destination displays painted out. (Kingston upon Hull History Centre)

Also seen in July 1943 is a Daimler CO5G with Weymann body at the Dairycoates level crossing, working service 3 to Pickering Park. (Kingston upon Hull History Centre)

The AEC 'Q' is seen here with other buses collecting school children from Hall Road Primary School in 1942. It was withdrawn in July 1943. (Kingston upon Hull History Centre)

Not a very good photograph but it shows the
use of one of several snow ploughs used by
the Transport Department. No. 191 is bound
for the small village of Wawne, which then
involved a long rural journey. It is still in original
condition but has received the standard livery.
(Authors' collection)

Guy Arab No. 228 is believed to have been diverted from Cardiff Corporation along with No. 229. Its Park
Royal UH56R body was retained until withdrawal in 1953. (East Pennine Transport Group)

AEC Regent No. 190 is at rest alongside the remains of the Central Bus Garage having received full standard livery. It would soon receive the Massey body from AEC Regent No. 180, only three years its senior. (J. Fozard)

AEC Regent No. 196 has received a full repaint with the straight rectangle containing 'CORPORATION TRANSPORT'. It will soon exchange bodies with Regent No. 173 and would survive until March 1953. (Authors' collection)

A post-war view in the Coach Station of 1939 AEC Regent No. 170 complete with its Massey body, which will soon be transferred to No. 191. (East Pennine Transport Group)

AEC Regent No. 197 with original Northern Counties H56R body is still in its 1942 condition, complete with full pre-war blind. It is seen at the Setting Dyke terminus in November 1947. It was later rebuilt by the Yorkshire Equipment Company of Bridlington in 1948 (compare with the photograph on page 44). (Authors' collection)

Guy Arab No. 235 of 1945 also retained its original Massey body until withdrawal in 1957. (R. F. Mac)

Hull's first post-war buses were sixteen AEC Regent IIs with Weymann H60R bodies. All arrived in the late summer of 1946. No. 255 is seen at Wymersley Road in February 1954. Withdrawal came in 1966. (A. Cross)

Not all the Coach Station terminal stands were under the canopy, as can be seen with this rear view of Weymann-bodied AEC Regent III No. 289. The shelters were painted green and each (including those under the canopy) showed the service numbers and destination/via points in black on white within a standard panel. (Authors' collection)

Each year in October the week-long Hull Fair (the country's largest) was held. This involved a large number of extra journeys on bus and trolleybus routes in the evenings and on the last Saturday. This view on Spring Bank West shows two Guy Arabs led by No. 238 parked waiting for their next journey while a Massey-bodied AEC Regent is working an extra service 11 journey to Wymersley Road. (R. F. Mack)

A daily scene witnessed by Malcolm on his way to school. The 'Fish Dock Bus', as the 26/27 services were known, is Regent No. 196, which is travelling along St George's Road towards Anlaby Road. It would have started at West Dock Avenue, adjoining the Fish Dock (St Andrew's Dock), about five minutes earlier and is working the off peak 26 as far as De Grey Street. The body is from Regent No. 173. Malcolm caught the 7:50 a.m. service 27 to Bankside as far as Princes Avenue each school day (sometimes with seconds to spare!). (Authors' collection)

Until the one way system was introduced in June 1964, all inward northern and some eastern bus routes travelled three quarters of a circle around the war memorial in Paragon Square. Guy Arab No. 209, with body from Daimler No. 19 and new standard destination layout, will shortly reach the Coach Station. (East Pennine Transport Group)

Leyland TD7 No. 200 with all-metal Leyland body to Western SMT Co. Ltd specification stands at the service 50 barrier in the Coach Station. The Leylands were practically unaltered until withdrawal in March 1960. (East Pennine Transport Group)

Guy Arab No. 213 is thought to have received the Northern Counties body from either 1942 AEC Regent No. 198 or 199, the body being rebuilt by the Corporation. It has just left the Central Bus Garage. (Authors' collection)

AEC Regent No. 262 was delivered in May 1947 and carried a Weymann H58R body. It is seen here at the Stoneferry Green terminus of service 30, which was the terminus of the original 1909 route. The whole area has changed today, although a few houses have survived. No. 262 was retired in January 1967. (Authors' collection)

Guy Arab No. 232 leaves the Preston Road stand in the bus station with a full load (not unusual for this service). It has the Massey body from AEC Regent No. 189 and was one of the last Arabs to be withdrawn in March 1963. (R. F. Mack)

For many years the Newbridge Road buses were routed via New Cross Street and Queens Gardens rather than the whole of Alfred Gelder Street. AEC Regent No. 275 is in New Cross Street. (J. Fozard)

Eight feet wide, AEC Regent III No. 333 of 1950 is doing good business on Bricknell Avenue en route to York Road. It has a Weymann H58R body. Retirement came at the end of 1969. (G. M. O'Connell)

Guy Arab No. 215 with original Park Royal UH56R body passes what was then the new Co-operative building in Jameson Street. It was withdrawn in June 1960. (Authors' collection)

A full Coach Station but with not many passengers. This picture gives a good view of the stands which were not under the canopy. (Authors' collection)

AEC Regent III No. 270 at work on Willerby Road on the 12, which branched off to Wold Road. It ran from May 1947 to January 1968. (Authors' collection)

The arrival of ten AEC Reliances – Nos 157–166 – in 1957 enabled services 14 (Bricknell Avenue) and 19 (Sutton Road/Leads Road) to become one-man operated. Weymann B40D bodies were fitted, later reduced to B39D to permit more standing passengers to be carried. It is seen on Beverley High Road en route to Sutton Road. No. 157 (renumbered 57 in 1967) was taken out of service in 1975 and was reputedly sold to ATS Lagos by a dealer. All were converted to automatic monocontrol. (Authors' collection)

Consecutively numbered AEC Regents Nos 316 and 317 are caught at the shops on Bricknell Avenue in 1958. The driver of No. 317 has his sliding door open. (J. Fozard)

AEC Regent II No. 250 is about to reach Cottingham Road Garage after working on service 19. This photograph was taken by Les Storry who worked at the garage for many years. (L. R. Storry)

The original Drypool Bridge across the River Hull was very narrow until rebuilt in the late 1950s. AEC Regent No. 243 has experienced a rare working on the 49 (Hedon), which was normally the preserve of EYMS. (A. B. Cross)

This shows the flap on the pre-war destination display in the up position to reveal the 'CITY' destination. I don't remember ever seeing this being used in service. (R. F. Mack)

Possibly a unique view of both front and rear of the 1953 AEC Regent IIIs with handsome Weymann H58R bodies, seen in Holderness Road garage yard. No. 339 is festooned with advertisements. (J. Fozard)

AEC Regent III No. 326 with a handsome Weymann H58R body leads a large collection of buses and trolleybuses along Carr Lane en route for the Coach Station. The rear ends of these buses needed large-scale repairs in the early 1960s, some of which was carried out by Charles A. Roe. (J. Fozard)

AEC Regent II No. 262 waits for No. 267 to cross Drypool Bridge in 1951. Note the road surface. (Authors' collection)

In May 1960, AEC Regent No. 197 prepares to leave Cottingham Road garage (by the entrance door!) (Compare with the photograph on page 32). (Malcolm Wells)

The appearance in service of the five Leyland Atlanteans in June 1960 caused a stir. Malcolm rode on No. 342 on 1 June en route to school (stop outside the school entrance). The MCCW bodies were of H75F configuration while they introduced three-track route number blinds. Service 22 was chosen for the Atlanteans because its stand adjoined the railway station so that they would not block any other stands. The location is Cottingham Road near Newland Avenue with Billy Williams at the helm. Note the bus stop sign complete with fare stage bar. (L. R. Storry)

On 29 January 1961, ten Atlanteans (Nos 347–356) replaced trolleybuses on service 70 to Dairycoates. This was Hull's most profitable route. Both Atlanteans have just arrived from the city centre and will turn via the turning area at the top of Dairycoates Road. The Roe bodies did not meet the usual elegance associated with the company. (Authors' collection)

A deserted Paragon Street at night with Atlantean No. 354 at the service 70 barrier and a Roe-bodied Sunbeam W at the 69 barrier. (R. F. Mack)

Between August and November 1961, ten former Newcastle Corporation Daimler CVG6s entered service. Ostensibly to assist with the conversion of trolleybus services 61/65, they worked bus routes because problems with the Weymann bodies on AEC Regent IIIs caused many to be taken out of service for attention by the Corporation's own workshops and Charles H. Roe. No. 129 had MCCW H55R bodywork, as did eight others – the other being by Roe. The location is Spring Bank. (Authors' collection)

Nos 124 and 128 were fitted with a removable hatch for tuition purposes. The driver here is the late Mac Staveley, at that time a motorman on trolleybuses. He later became chairman of the Transport Committee and Chair of the privatised Hull City Transport Ltd. No. 128 is a credit to Arthur Robson's paint shop and is leaving Cottingham Road garage. (L. R. Storry)

The second trolleybus conversion (Nos 69 and 71) took place on 4 February 1962. Twelve Atlanteans were allocated to Wheeler Street garage for the service. The exit from the garage immediately behind the level crossing was very tight. (Authors' collection)

A nice side view of AEC Regent No. 190 in its last year of service as it turns from Anlaby Road into Ferensway on service 43. (G. R. Mills)

The former trolleybus short working (No. 71), which was used mainly for Hull RLFC matches, was renumbered 269. Ex-Newcastle Daimler No. 121 is seen resting in Selby Street until the end of a game. (Malcolm Wells)

The tenth former Newcastle Daimler carried a Roe H56R body and was one year older than the rest, having originally entered service in 1947. No. 130 was withdrawn in January 1967, the remainder going in December 1966 or January 1967. The location is the Central Garage yard with the new office block (and an ex-St Helens RT) behind. (Authors' collection)

An unidentified AEC Regent III negotiates the road works involved with the replacement of the Dairycoates level crossing with a road bridge ('Flyover' in Hull parlance). (Authors' collection)

A trio of rear ends in Queen Victoria Square. The nearest is AEC Regent III No. 297, which is returning from the Corporation Pier. (Authors' collection)

The first day (Sunday) of the replacement service 18 for the last trolleybus service, 63. Brand new Atlantean No. 402 with driver Tom Ushcroft and his conductor Charlie Kaye is posing for the camera at Cottingham Road garage. (L. R. Storry)

In September 1963, as part of a general renumbering exercise, the 11 was altered to 81, as seen on Regent No. 252, which is inward bound near Seagrave Grove. Note the cream and green telephone box of the city owned telephone system in the background. (J. Fozard)

With the arrival of seven Leyland Panthers (Nos 172 to 178), circular services 101/102 became a seven days a week operation. No. 172 was exhibited at the 1964 Commercial Motor Show and had a loan session in Southport. The route was amended in north Hull due to the longer (35 feet) length of the saloons. The location is Greenwood Avenue. In 1966 it was renumbered 72. (Authors' collection)

Panther No. 173 shows off it Roe B45F (later B44F) dual door body at the service 14 Bricknell Avenue terminus. (Authors' collection)

On 3 April 1966, AEC Regent III No. 311 stands at the Newland Avenue terminus of service 20. This was previously the terminus of trolleybus service 62. (Malcolm Wells)

Another former trolleybus terminus was Endike Lane (service 63). AEC Regent No. 275 is about take on a large number of passengers before departing for Chapel Street. No. 275 was withdrawn in January 1968. The scene is pretty much the same today. (Malcolm Wells)

In 1962 nineteen RT-type AEC Regents were bought from St Helens (numbered 131 to 149). Their lack of saloon heating was not appreciated by local passengers. Here No. 135 stands at Newland Avenue in April 1966. (Malcolm Wells)

It was unusual to see an AEC Regal work on the Fish Dock Bus route but on 8 March 1968 No. 154 (ex-No. 4 and later No. 54) awaits departure time in De Grey Street. The Weymann B35F body was a neat one which absorbed the destination display quite well. New in 1949, it was withdrawn in 1970 – a creditable length of service. (Malcolm Wells)

More second-hand buses arrived in 1966. These were twelve AEC Regent IIIs from Leicester numbered 201 to 212. New in 1949, the Brush bodies were re-seated from H60R to H59R before entry into service in Hull. No. 205 had entered service in June 1966, two months before this view at Endike Lane on 10 August 1966. They were renumbered 101 to 112 in December 1966. (Malcolm Wells)

AEC Regent III No. 334 is about to turn from Chapel Street into Paragon Street while working the trolleybus replacement service 23. (J. Fozard)

By 26 January 1967, when this picture was taken, the former Hessle Road trolleybus service had been extended to Gipsyville and the 73 to Boothferry Estate, which also ran via Hessle Road, had been diverted along Paragon Street. No. 372 dates from March 1963 while No. 215 is less than one month old. The contrast between the two styles of Roe bodywork is revealing. (Malcolm Wells)

Ex-St Helens RT No. 135 has just reversed into the lay by at the Sutton Road terminus on 9 June 1967. Houses and industrial units surround this area now. (Malcolm Wells)

AEC Reliance No. 66 (ex-166) rests in Short Street on 9 June 1967, just one month after the first routes to the Bransholme Estate were introduced. No. 66 carries the destination 'WAWNE ESTATE', which was the short-lived original name for the estate. The 32A ran via Stoneferry while the 34A worked via Holderness Road. (Malcolm Wells)

AEC Reliance No. 161 (renumbered No. 61 later in the month) stands at De Grey Street on 4 February 1967. Note the large 'PAY AS YOU ENTER' sign. (Malcolm Wells)

On 11 May 1967, AEC Regent III No. 294 stands at the James Reckitt Avenue terminus of service 40. In the background a Leyland Panther is eastbound on the circular 101. (Malcolm Wells)

Service 40 was extended from James Reckitt Avenue to Wembley Park Avenue on 20 August 1967. No. 279 is pictured there on 21 September 1967. (Malcolm Wells)

Leyland Panther No. 76 (ex-176) collects passengers on Leads Road on 21 September 1967. (Malcolm Wells)

The central doorway of AEC Reliance No. 163 (later No. 63) is in use to permit passengers to disembark near Endike Lane on Beverley Road. Despite the destination display, No. 163 is inward bound for the city centre. The Cross Keys pub across the road is still alive and well. (Malcolm Wells)

Leyland Atlanteans 213 to 257 carried a more rounded Roe H75F body, more in keeping with traditional Roe designs. No. 229 was new in January 1968 and is seen here at the Saner Street stop on Anlaby Road opposite the EYMS head offices, with George Mellors at the wheel. (Authors' collection)

No. 219 has just entered Beverley Road from Greenwood Avenue en route to the Coach Station, despite the destination display. It was common practice (if not policy) not to re-set the blind – a result of not having to reset under the previous system. The date is 1 August 1968. (Malcolm Wells)

In a bid to retain passengers from the west, the Hessle Road (70) and Anlaby Road (67/69) terminus stands were transferred to Guildhall Road from Paragon Street. This area had not seen regular journeys to and from west Hull. Atlantean No. 142 (ex-342) stands at the 69 barrier with a Reliance and the College of Technology behind. (Malcolm Wells)

Between 1967 and 1969 thirty-six AEC Regents with Park Royal H56R bodies were acquired from Nottingham Corporation. This is No. 152, which stands in the middle of a partly built Bransholme. No. 152 served Hull from April 1967 until December 1971. (Authors' collection)

Most of the AEC Regent IIIs received the three-track number blind arrangement at the front, as shown here on No. 339 on Hessle Road near Liverpool Street. The three smaller numbers upset the balance of the design. The shops to the left of No. 339 still remain but the others were demolished a long time ago. (Malcolm Wells)

The 1966 batch of Atlanteans differed from previous Roe bodywork in having the flat windscreen, as shown here. No. 412 (later 212) is at the Orchard Park terminus on 19 May 1968 with the high-rise flats under construction in the background, all of which have since been demolished!. (Authors' collection)

No. 247 entered service in December 1968 and remained at work until August 1990, which was a creditable length of service. It carried a Union Jack livery from May 1977 to March 1978 to commemorate the Queen's Silver Jubilee, being numbered temporarily 25. (Authors' collection)

Ex-Nottingham No. 168 is seen on Willerby Road working service 81. Several Nottingham buses received a smaller route number indicator as seen here. It entered service in January 1969 and was subsequently fitted with a removable hatch for driver tuition purposes. Withdrawal came in November 1972. Another 'Nottingham' is across the road. (Authors' collection)

December 1969 saw most of the 258–277 batch of Atlanteans entering service on the northern routes from Cottingham Road garage. They carried a new and attractive (in the eyes of both authors) Roe body design with long windows and to H71D capacity. No. 274 is seen in April 1970 at the Ellerburn Avenue terminus of service 22. (Malcolm Wells)

Conductor Len Ogle poses for the camera as he prepares to work the last crew-operated journey on service 69 on Friday 10 November 1972 at 17:15 from Meadowbank Road back into the city centre, thus making KHCT the first major urban operator to achieve 100 per cent One-Man Operation. (Authors' collection)

Atlantean No. 177 (ex-377) passes St James' Church in Sutton in the autumn of 1973 en route for Wawne. By now the near side destination display above the first lower deck window had been painted over. It was withdrawn in June 1980. (Malcolm Wells)

No. 258 is seen here on its first day in service, 1 December 1969, at the Tweendykes Road terminus at Ings Road. (Authors' collection)

From 1971 the bodywork on the Atlanteans reverted to single door and H72F configuration. No. 309 was captured on 12 October 1972 in Paragon Street at the former service 70 terminus. This batch (Nos 298 to 317) was the last to carry the streamlined livery. It was sold to Fylde Borough Council in September 1986 and was withdrawn in 1996. (Authors' collection)

A fine view of Atlantean No. 318 (Hull's first AN68) in the revised livery, as shown at the Commercial Motor Show in September 1972. (G. M. O'Connell)

Two of the 1969 dual door Atlanteans side by side in the Coach Station. No. 276 is crew-operated while No. 262 is driver-operated, as can be seen by the Solomatic ticket machine for use on the recent OMO conversion of the Orchard Park routes. (Authors' collection)

St James Church in Sutton watches as No. 306 passes en route to Saltshouse Road. It was transferred to the Citilink fleet in November 1990 before sale to Fylde in September 1992. (J. Fozard)

A fine side view of No. 290 in the Coach Station with the nearside blind still in use. The small 'C' under the fleet number shows that is was allocated to Cottingham Road garage. 'H' was Holderness Road but Central buses did not carry a letter. No. 290 was taken out of service in July 1986. (Authors' collection)

No. 146 (ex-346) prepares to cross Boothferry Road from North Road on works service 71W – one of many that was introduced in the 1960s. The floodlights belong to the then Boothferry Park, home of Hull City AFC. No. 146 was sold to West Midlands PTE in October 1975, who withdrew it in June 1977. (Malcolm Wells)

Some journeys were operated for workers at the Birds Eye factory in Gipsyville. Atlantean No. 145 (ex-345) awaits departure time along with another Atlantean. No. 145 has managed to acquire a 'Shop at Binns' advertisement under the destination box. It was also sold to West Midlands PTE after service in Hull. (Malcolm Wells)

Having originally been allocated to Cottingham Road garage, Atlantean No. 198 (ex-398) had graduated to Holderness Road by 1973 when this view was taken. It is bound for Bransholme. Withdrawal came in January 1981. (Malcolm Wells)

To celebrate the 80th anniversary of the undertaking, No. 252 was painted in the tramways' crimson lake and broken white livery in July 1979. It is seen later that year on a school working to Orchard Park. A return to standard livery came two years later. Withdrawal came in August 1990. (Malcolm Wells)

The department lost patience with Leyland and bought thirty Scania Metropolitans with MCCW bodywork in 1975–78. No. 414 is working a school service on Anlaby Road. Its working life with Hull was short, being withdrawn in 1987. (Malcolm Wells)

The Transport Department built up a large number of schools services, as seen here with No. 249 blocking traffic on Priory Road as it collects students. No. 249 was taken out of service in July 1990. (Malcolm Wells)

When the Ings Road Estate was built two routes were opened, the 55 to the west and the 57 to the east. Atlantean No. 241, which stands at the 57 terminus, was withdrawn in 1985. (Malcolm Wells)

In 1982 KHCT launched what was to become a sizeable coach fleet branded 'KINGSTONIAN', each carrying a name. No. 22, a Leyland/Plaxton C51F, was a member of the original trio and named *William Wilberforce*. It was transferred to York Pullman from November 1990 until January 1994. (Authors' collection)

In later years the coaching fleet could be found in the open behind Liverpool Street workshops. No. 56 was a Volvo/Plaxton C53FT combination of 1990. It was sold along with the rest of the coaching fleet to East Yorkshire in 1997. (Malcolm Wells)

Metropolitan No. 433 was formerly Merseyside PTE No. 4033. It is seen here newly repainted in Liverpool Street in September 1974. It was withdrawn as part of the wholesale withdrawals in July 1986. (Malcolm Wells)

In 1976 five Ford /Tricentrol B23Fs were acquired for a city centre route. They were not successful and were withdrawn in 1981. No. 13 is at the Corporation Pier. (Malcolm Wells)

Metropolitan No. 419 is working a Guildhall journey on the 73D from Boothferry Easter. It is loading passengers on Hessle Road opposite Rugby Street. No. 419 was withdrawn in 1987. (Malcolm Wells)

An unidentified Atlantean picking up passengers in a typical Bransholme townscape. (Malcolm Wells)

The small village of Wawne graduated from a few (mostly market days) journeys per week to an hourly service via North Bransholme. No. 326 has just reversed into Greens Lane from Ferry Lane, a manoeuvre still extant in 2017. No. 326 was withdrawn in 1987. (Malcolm Wells)

In September 1968, the 55 and 58 were linked to form a circular route. Metropolitan No. 424 is awaiting departure in Diadem Grove amid typical Corporation housing. (Malcolm Wells)

This circular service 33C to Bransholme along James Reckitt Avenue was essentially the Garden Village route extended to Bransholme District Centre. No. 252 is seen here during 1983. (Malcolm Wells)

Metropolitan No. 421 heads south along Chanterlands Avenue on the 15C, having come from Orchard Park. No. 421 had a short working life of ten years, being withdrawn in early 1988. (Malcolm Wells)

With a rather sloppy blind arrangement, Atlantean No. 246 works a morning peak journey from Orchard Park along Bricknell Avenue in 1983. It was sold together with No. 244 to local operator Connor & Graham Ltd in October 1990 and was acquired by EYMS when it purchased the company in 1991. (Malcolm Wells)

A trio of buses awaiting the school bell at Bricknell Avenue (Kelvin Hall). No. 246 will work the 15:55 to Mizzen Road via Cottingham Road and Beverley Road. (Malcolm Wells)

A late evening shot of No. 356 in the Coach Station. No. 356 was withdrawn in December 1985. (Authors' collection)

In 1989 No. 137 was repainted in the tramway livery to celebrate ninety years of municipal transport. It is seen on Beverley Road about to be overtaken by a Kingstonian coach. (Malcolm Wells)

The high-rise flats tower over Atlantean No. 337 as it leaves the Orchard Park bus terminus. No. 337 was transferred to Citilink in August 1990 but was withdrawn in November. (J. Fozard)

Another peak working is about to be worked by No. 354 at Bransholme Centre. The centre was (and is) the hub for most of buses to and from the city centre. It is thought that No. 354 was the first to receive a total re-spray in lieu of the usual KHCT approach. Some sources say it went to Citilink but former KHCT employees dispute this. (Malcolm Wells)

No. 257 stands in Mizzen Road, part of what was popularly known as the Ghost Estate when it was first built. It wears the revised 1984 livery. Transferred to Citilink from June 1990 until April 1993, No. 257 was withdrawn in April 1994 – a life of twenty-six years. (Malcolm Wells)

A brand new Metrobus No. 508 enters the Coach Station on 24 March 1980. The livery could look very smart in this condition and stands comparison with any modern-day colours. Withdrawal came in September 1994. (Malcolm Wells)

Metrobus No. 501 is working on what had become the Outer Circle when caught in St George's Road. After withdrawal in 1994 it was converted to open top in the fleet of London Pride Sightseeing Ltd. (Malcolm Wells)

Another peak works service was the 71W, seen here being worked by Metropolitan No. 421 in North Road. By now the traditional KHCT bus stops had succumbed to the national (and boring) standard. (Malcolm Wells)

On the very edge of Noddle Hill Way on the Bransholme Estate is Atlantean No. 371, which was a part of the last batch bought by Hull in 1981. (D. Longbottom)

A view of the solid rear end of Metropolitan No. 406 on Anlaby High Road. No. 406 was withdrawn in November 1986 – a life of just eleven years. (Malcolm Wells)

No. 321 passes Holy Trinity Church on a morning peak working of the 35D from Bransholme which was routed via the Market Place and Old Town. Transfer to Citilink came in June 1991 and York Pullman in September 1992, where it was subsequently withdrawn. (Malcolm Wells)

An afternoon school special sees No. 272 in Greenwood Avenue working to Bransholme. It was withdrawn in July 1987. (Malcolm Wells)

Full time at Boothferry Park sees No. 348 about to work a special to Bilton Grange (42X). Compare the two versions of the post-streamline livery. No. 348 was damaged by fire in September 1986 and withdrawn. (Malcolm Wells)

Ex-Merseyside PTE No. 431 rests near Rokeby Avenue in Anlaby Park Road North on the Boothferry Estate circular 63C. No. 431 was a deregulation casualty in July 1986 and was sold in February 1987. (Malcolm Wells)

Yarmouth Avenue on Boothferry Estate is the location for this view of 348. Alternate buses terminated here while the 73C continued to Rokeby Avenue. It was damaged by a fire in September 1986 and sold to Camms. (Malcolm Wells)

Atlantean No. 302 stands at the then limit of Bransholme construction, ready to work a 32B back to the city. (Malcolm Wells)

The Chanterlands Avenue North terminus was always short of passengers, even in tram and trolleybus days. Here is No. 249 on a 26 working. After a long life it was withdrawn in July 1990. (Malcolm Wells)

Holderness Road garage closed in July 1986 when the drastic fleet reduction took place after the large route reorganisation was introduced. It contained several withdrawn buses led by former resident No. 308. This remained with KHCT Ltd until April 1988 when it was sold to Fylde. (Malcolm Wells)

The Garden Village route ran through the housing built by Reckitts for its workers, having been started in March 1923. Sixty-four years later Atlantean No. 270 (now beautifully preserved) sports the final bus livery on route 9 (Bransholme). (Authors' collection)

The 'Avenues' were an expensive and attractive place to live and its residents fought against the bus route, albeit unsuccessfully. Dominator No. 106 was new in October 1984 and was among those taken over by Cleveland Transit in 1993. (Malcolm Wells)

In later years the circular service was diverted outside the city boundary to the ASDA store in Bilton. This Marfleet bound Metrobus is about to turn into the supermarket's approach road. (Malcolm Wells)

In January 1987 fifteen Fiat 49-10s with Robin Hood B25F bodies were placed in service on three new routes that served areas of the city away from the main radial routes. No. 605 is caught in Woodcock Street on the 39 with George Millington at the wheel. The end came in July 1996. (Malcolm Wells)

In 1985 a Leyland National with dual door bodywork was placed in service. The centre door had a lift for wheelchairs. It was called 'Handirider', running on specific routes on each day, and was painted in what was almost the Kingstonian livery. It had its own stand behind the offices in the Coach Station and the lift is seen in use in this view, supervised by driver Tom Owston. It was withdrawn in June 1999 after transfer to Cleveland Transit. (Malcolm Wells)

In September 1986, KHCT Ltd found itself short of serviceable buses to meet the large number of school contracts that it won. It acquired eight Atlanteans with Alexander H76D bodies which entered service in October, still in West Yorkshire PTE livery complete with ex-Bradford fleet numbers. Two can be seen inside Cottingham Road garage in late 1986. Metropolitan No. 414 was one of several buses reinstated for school contract work, hence the 77S route number. (Malcolm Wells)

Another interior post-deregulation view of Cottingham Road garage with a variety of models and liveries. (Malcolm Wells)

Slowly but surely the WYPTE Atlanteans received standard livery. No. 466 is seen outside the Ice Arena alongside the retail park on the short-lived 610 to and from Bransholme. All had the centre door sealed in 1988. No. 466 was withdrawn in August 1990 and sold to Fylde. (Malcolm Wells)

As part of the 90th anniversary celebrations in 1989 Dominator No. 135 received the former trolleybus livery. It is seen here leaving George Street bound for the Coach Station. (Malcolm Wells)

Five minutes after seeing No. 135, sister No. 136 came along. This wore the 1932 Duncan Morrison bus livery. Despite the destination blind it is bound for the Coach Station. (Malcolm Wells)

Atlantean No. 351 carries the Citilink white livery for school contracts but still has its original fleet number. Seen outside the Central Library in Prospect Street, it is working on a main route 2 to Boothferry Estate. (Malcolm Wells)

The post-deregulation school contracts took KHCT into previously unexplored territory. Citilink No. C5 is seen in Beverley Bus Station with St Mary's Church in the background. The driver is Dave Coster. (Malcolm Wells)

Citilink No. C3, in the charge of driver Derek Sims, picks up passengers on Bilton Grange Estate on the 644 – one of the former independent Citilink's routes. (Malcolm Wells)

Scania No. 816 of 1990 leaves the Coach Station on one of the many Bransholme routes. No. 816 was sold to First Manchester in 2000. (Authors' collection)

Rather than work empty after delivering a school working some journeys were registered on existing (usually EYMS) routes. Dominator No. 155 (later 255) is seen in Main Street, Cherry Burton, on such a trip. (Malcolm Wells)

When buses were returned to the main fleet from Citilink not all were immediately repainted. Some, like No. 257, received a blue and white front. The 'Blue and Whites' slogan was part of a large scale promotion. The location is Willerby Road near Manor Road. (Malcolm Wells)

Scania saloon No. 701 is seen at Cottingham Green awaiting departure to Hull. This was one of several routes in 1992 on which KHCT competed with EYMS. (Malcolm Wells)

Working for the main fleet is Dominator No. 113, which is approaching Hessle Square on the extended service 15. (Malcolm Wells)

Still carrying the 'YORK PULLMAN' fleet name, Atlantean No. 365 is back with the main fleet and working on route 11 to Bransholme. (Authors' collection)

Paul Morfitt stands alongside Atlantean C2 before working his final day with Citilink on Friday 28 August 1992 before the company was transferred back to full KHCT operation the following week. (Authors' collection)

The 1992 competition saw Hull's buses reach Anlaby (once a dream of the Tramways Committee) with Dominator No. 129 collecting custom opposite the Red Lion. This is our last view of the blue and white that lit up drab winter days. (Malcolm Wells)